What Happens in the End?

PHILIP RUGE-JONES

BASIC QUESTIONS

Augsburg Fortress, Minneapolis

Contents

BASIC QUESTIONS
What Happens in the End? Learner Book
This learner book has a corresponding leader guide.

Editors: Katherine A. Evensen and Douglas Schmitz
Series design: Lois Stanfield, LightSource Images
Cover and interior art: Greg Lewis Studios

Scripture quotations are from New Revised Standard Version Bible, copyright © 1989
Division of Christian Education of the National Council of the Churches of Christ in the
United States of America. Used by permission.

ISBN 0-8066-3817-6

Manufactured in U.S.A.
1 2 3 4 5 6 7 8 9 0 1 2 3 4 5 6 7 8 9

The Millennium

*We do not know the date of
the end, but Jesus teaches us how
to live faithfully while waiting.*

MARK 13:32-37
JESUS' WARNING AND PROMISE

Jesus was sure that God was taking creation somewhere. He knew difficult times would come to his followers, but that God would not abandon them. The timing of the end was not theirs to know. In fact, neither the angels nor Jesus himself knew what God's timing would be. Yet knowing the "when" of the ending was not important. In the love that Jesus had shown his followers they had seen the heart of God. For Jesus stood before them as God's Son and representative. In Jesus, they had learned that God comes to them in love to nourish and heal them. Because they knew "who" would achieve the end, they could wait for it in faith without worrying about "when" this would happen.

The timing of the end always has been source of curiosity for Christians. Throughout the history of the church, especially during times of crisis, people have believed that surely they lived in the last times. As Christians approached the end of the first millennium, some were convinced that God would break in and establish the kingdom of God then and there. Something about those three zeros in a row made them think that the moment was pregnant with possibility. As the western world approaches the year 2000, similar suspicions abound. Perhaps this will be the moment when God finally interrupts the corrupt rhythms that rock our lives between hope and despair!

Fascination with numbers is not limited to the end of each calender millennium. Whole systems of thought have been based upon symbolic numbers mined from the bible. If you tune into a Christian radio station, you may hear talk of the "millennium" mentioned in the last book of the bible. The book of Revelation, some of which we will explore in our next session, speaks of "a thousand years" when the saints of God will reign with their Lord. Moving out of this solitary biblical text (Revelation 20:1-7), some Christians have made "millennialism" a centerpiece of their faith. Part of the challenge for such Christians has been figuring out exactly when this reign would occur. Current events become mathematical clues to the timing of the end. The prophets of old were speaking directly about events in our day: the forming of the United Nations, the conflicts in the Middle East, the downfall of international communism. These all are seen as the keys that open up the secrets of the end.

In such a context, Jesus speaks to us again, reminding us that no one knows the day or the hour. He stands against those who would nail down with mathematical precision the time when God will be all in all. We can trust that Jesus will not reveal in a cryptic way to a small group of people what he told his disciples he himself did not know.

Jesus also challenges those who have been lulled to sleep by the long period of waiting. If the spiritual mathematicians have the timing wrong, they do not miss on the issue of urgency. God may indeed come tomorrow, so keep awake.

This was Jesus' point in our biblical text. He tells us who will usher in the end (God), and then calls us to be alert. He reminds us of the end for which we have been created. Jesus tells us that we live in a world that belongs to God and that we are to take care of this "house" as though it belonged to another. We are to live as God's creatures taking care of the creation in which God has placed us. We are to recognize that God is the "master" of the "house" into which we have been placed.

Martin Luther, the man for whom the Lutheran church was eventually named, lived in the sixteenth century. Many of his contemporaries saw in odd weather conditions or in animals born with strange deformities signs that the end was near. Luther was willing to believe that the end very well might occur at any moment. Yet he differed from his contemporaries in the way he responded to this possibility. While most believed that the appropriate way to respond to the approaching end was to become more rigorous in religious exercises, Luther offered another interpretation.

Luther went back to the beginning of God's original act of creation. When the first human beings were created, God commanded them to take care of the garden paradise that surrounded them and to be fruitful and multiply (Genesis 1:28). Martin Luther is rumored to have said that if God should return tomorrow, Luther hoped to be found serving the end for which God had created him. Luther's earthy desire was to be found by God planting a tree or expressing his love for his wife, Katie, in their marital bed.

This is a strikingly biblical understanding of how we are to live as creatures of God. Knowing that we are created by God, we turn to the rest of creation and tend to its needs. We are to be "stewards" or caretakers of what is not our own. Since God loves the whole creation, we are to heal the groanings of that same creation on God's behalf. This is the chief end or goal that should occupy our lives as God's good creatures. In living as God created us to live, we bring glory to God.

The glory of God is reflected among us when we plant a tree or love those who have been placed in our lives. We glorify God when we live together as God has intended from the beginning. The one who will bring the end is the same one who gave us our beginning. Faithfulness means keeping alert to the words and world that this one calls to our attention. We are not to escape from this world, but to love it with God.

PHILIPPIANS 2:1-11
THE SHAPE OF FAITHFUL WAITING

This beautiful text was written by the apostle Paul. He took what may have been a much-loved hymn in his church and asked about the song's meaning for the community's life together.

Three movements in this text call for our attention. The tone of the first movement is set by the word "if" in verse 1. Next, verses 2-5 speak of what should happen if the preceding "if" is true. Finally, the text breaks out into song about Christ and what he has done. Let us look at these sections in turn.

The word "if" suggests what is unsure in our lives. Because of its inherent instability, we cannot really build our future on an "if." We may hope that a promise will be fulfilled, but "if" offers no security. From our childhood until our death, the ifs that meet us, cast us back on our own selves and our own resources: "*If* you clean your room, then you may go to your friend's house." "*If* you can change your ways, then I will consider marrying you."

At other times, "if" indicates something totally out of our control: "*If* it is not raining, then you will go to the park." "*If* I get that raise, then I will finally pay off the debt." These kinds of "ifs" leave us waiting for an uncertain future; it may or may not ever come. Spiritually, we have been left at times with that same conditional word: "*If* you do this, then God will take you to heaven." "*If* you are obedient, then God will bless you." "*If* you change your ways, then God will love you." The life of faith is unsure and precarious when all we have is an "if" to build upon.

Beginning verse 1 with the word "if" throws a big question mark upon all of the phrases that follow. With "if" standing in the way, we cannot trust that "there is any encouragement in Christ, any consolation in love, any sharing in the Spirit, any compassion and sympathy" (Philippians 2:1). All these things would be nice to have, but "if" leaves us hoping, like the child dreaming of the park. It sounds good, but maybe the clouds are rolling in.

Thus we begin our second movement without any confidence that what has gone before is true. We contemplate building our house, unsure if we can even secure the land upon which we would build. The second verse depends upon the fulfilling of the condition of that first "if." Until "what might be possible" is known by us as fact, we cannot really move forward. We are immobile until something can be done to clear up the uncertainty left by the first verse.

Finally, this comes to us when Paul starts singing of Christ's journey to us (2:6-11). Paul tells of Jesus Christ, who is one with God. As such, all power in heaven—the power that keeps the cosmos moving—was in his hands. Yet he let it go, emptied himself of it all, and became human. Not content with this descent, he continued downward within the human community until he found himself in the company of those most despised in his society. He respected the disrespected by standing with them in their place and making it his own. Living in their place, he offered them encouragement, consolation, solidarity, and compassion.

Jesus stayed on that course until it brought him to the cross. The cross in Jesus' day was reserved for only two types of "criminals": rebels who sought the overthrow of the government and fugitive slaves. Within Jesus' own religious community, dying on a cross was a sign of rejection by God. The cross was a curse, and if you were hung on one, you deserved it. Jesus was crucified as a sinner in the eyes of his contemporaries.

Yet precisely this—the fact that Jesus chose to enter into the company of slaves, rebels and rejected sinners—brings God to glorify him. Jesus has not only attended God's good creation, as our last section described it; he has attended to that creation in the places where it was most clearly broken. Jesus brought healing to the open wounds of his day. So Paul says, "Therefore God also highly exalted him" (Philippians 2:9). The "therefore" points us back to the gracious descent of Christ as the grounds for the alternative verdict God renders on his behalf. Jesus presented the groans of God's creatures before the throne of God through his faithful presence with the broken people of his day; in turn, he also represents the will and word of God on God's behalf before those same people. In a sense, the charge against him that led to the cross—sedition—is finally true. He has overthrown the order of his day and our day. He destroys all the levels of status, whether political, social, or religious, that have been constructed, often in God's name. All are now one in Christ and freed from the old orders.

God has raised the very one who was rejected by all the social and religious conventions of his day. God offers an alternative interpretation of who Jesus is. The one declared false is now declared true. The one who was seen as having nothing as he died on the cross is really the one who holds everything in his hands. The one who was insulted and ridiculed on the cross becomes praised as the name above all names.

With Christ, the whole singing congregation is carried into the presence of God. In Christ, there is no longer rejection but only glory. As we sing his song, we become like him in the eyes of God. We are declared by God, for Jesus' sake, true sons and daughters of God; we are held by the one who holds all things. We are transformed from sinners into God's chosen, holy people.

Something interesting has happened in the reading of this text. You can only overcome the beginning uncertainty by looking ahead to the ending. Once you look at the final hymn, the "if" becomes "because." Because there is encouragement in Christ, consolation from his love, sharing in his Holy Spirit, compassion and sympathy, then we too can be of the same mind. The land has been bought; now we can begin building.

The grammar of this text is the grammar of Christian faith. We

Fast Facts The technical word for the anticipation of God's future in our present is *prolepsis*. Though you may never use the word, the promise it holds is fundamental. Our future is truly anticipated when God breaks into our present bearing future gifts. Supremely this is so (1) in baptism, where we are declared God's children; (2) in the Lord's supper, where we are forgiven and brought into communion with God and one another; (3) wherever we announce to each other what God has done for us in Christ.

must look to the end to see the encouragement and compassion that is ours in the middle of all life's uncertainty. Seeing the future end that God has destined us for in Christ, we are changed in the present. The one who was born, lived on earth, died, and was raised is the same one who will usher in our future. The shape of our future with God is the shape of Christ's embrace. Our future is present for us today. Knowing that we shall be made holy, we receive in hope the forgiveness of sin. Our future is sure, so we face life's uncertainties with confidence.

Focus on the Stories

Judith had longed to spend some time abroad. She wanted to learn about the lives of other people in order to understand herself better. She had applied for a program offered through her college to study for one year in India. She was overjoyed when she received a letter acknowledging her acceptance into the India program. As she anticipated her time oversees, she began to read everything she could get her hands on about India. She began classes in one of the main languages spoken there. She met with other students and with them dreamed of their time together in that new land. They gathered at a local Indian restaurant and accustomed their taste buds to the food that awaited them as they also listened to sitar music. Together they began to live in the future as though it were a present reality.

◆ How did the future shape the way that Judith and her new friends lived? Have you ever had such an experience?

◆ In what ways are these kinds of experiences like Christian hope?

◆ How does the church gather to live in the present as though it were the future?

◆ How might we think of baptism as a letter of acceptance from God?

◆ What meal do we share in order to begin to experience the final banquet?

Philippians 2:10-11 looks like a worship service. We can draw all this together by saying:

> *We gather as a baptized people to share a meal and*
> *hear a word that anticipate our future with God and*
> *shape our daily life with one another.*

For the Next Session

Think about what the people you know face as their most difficult struggles or challenges.

Closing

> *Gracious God, you know our past sins and our present straying.*
> *Make us so conscious of the eternal weight of glory you are*
> *preparing for us that we live today as though it is your tomorrow;*
> *through Jesus Christ. Amen*

The Apocalypse

When we are caught in life's struggles, God is present with us, bringing newness to life.

MARK 13:24-31
WHEN LIFE IS SHAKEN

In this same chapter of Mark's Gospel, Jesus spoke of human relationships breaking down, of "war and rumors of war" (13:7), and of brother betraying brother (13:12). In our reading, the chaos turns cosmic. The universe comes crashing down; all hope in God is shaken. When Jesus speaks of this total collapse, he is using "apocalyptic" images. God spoke through messengers in this way when the people of God were locked in a fierce battle between life and death, hope and despair. There are many, even now, who have lived through such experiences.

Before Daniel had joined the Lutheran church in New York, he had seen much suffering. He had endured a civil war in his own country, El Salvador. He was imprisoned and tortured for his role in the church. Many of his friends had been killed by the government forces. Daniel had seen things that shook his world, and even "the heavens were shaken" for him. Yet, he also knew faithful people who had dared to name the death-dealing evil that threatened his people and who sought to protect life in the name of the living God. He had come to believe that life was a struggle, but God was in the strife, seeking life for all. In places like El Salvador, apocalyptic images come alive, speaking boldly to people in their suffering.

Apocalyptic inspiration usually comes in situations like the one that Daniel had endured. When a community's life is threatened by political conflict or natural disaster, hope can be born anew in the strange images of the apocalyptic. Apocalyptic speech acknowledges that life is a struggle and moments arise when those who follow God's ways are attacked by those who defy God. In such times, the word of God takes a stand and calls a thing what it is. God does not mince words, but publicly challenges the evil and names the pain and sorrow of the people. The enemy of God is recognized as a "beast" who seeks to devour God's holy people.

During these dangerous times, an announcement that condemns powerful tyrants could easily invite retaliation. So the language is often highly symbolic and filled with bizarre images. Yet, the suffering people know who the all-consuming dragon is or that the seven-headed monster is the despot who robs their people of life. The troubled hearts of the people penetrate the odd images that name God's enemies. When God's representative stands and names the evil, it is the first step toward claiming that God is present and has heard the people's cry.

Yet, the claim of apocalyptic faith goes far beyond this. Often the earthly struggle is echoed by a battle in God's abode. "The powers in heaven will be shaken," Jesus says (Mark 13:25). In this way, the strange word is a promise that God has not abandoned the people and that the struggle is not theirs alone. God experiences the battle, not from a distance, but within God's own dwelling place. We are not abandoned! God suffers with us.

As the universe collapsed around Jesus' listeners, he

Fast Facts Apocalypse literally means "to reveal" or "to uncover." It indicates a form of literature which employs bizarre images to speak of God's relationship with history. The book of Revelation is the most extensive Christian apocalypse in the Bible. Other examples of this style of writing within the scriptures include: the entire book of Daniel, Ezekiel 38–39, Isaiah 24–27, Zechariah 12–14, and Joel 3.

announced that God was present in order to save. Jesus promised that his listeners would see the Son of Man, a code for himself as the "True Human Being," coming with power and glory upon the clouds. Though the heavens were shaken, the end was assured. God would be victorious. God chooses to enter into the battle and suffering, confidently promising that the victory will be won. The "words which will not pass away" (Mark 13:31) are words of promise. They assure us that life, not death, will have the final say.

This powerful language has been capable of lifting up beaten down communities of faith. The word of promise has drawn people together so that they could be signs of hope for each other. Daniel was lifted through his anger, confusion, and frustration when companions from his faith community stood beside him in the struggle. The reality of God's presence was made believable for Daniel through the life-seeking presence of brothers and sisters in Christ. Likewise, the hope offered in these strange texts became real for the original listeners as the word grasped their hearts in hope and drew them together for mutual support. They could face the tyrants, because the love and solidarity of God had taken on flesh in their own community.

At this point, we need to offer a word of caution. This kind of language has rarely been the standard way for the people of faith to confess their hope. The explosive images can be dangerous when handled outside of the Holy Spirit who inspires them. When we are honest, we recognize that our world rarely stands before God's judgment in clear divisions of "beasts" and "innocents." Usually the truth is much more muddy. This is not to deny the reality of evil and struggle or God's participation in the fray. It also does not deny that God will have the final victory. But this confession of complexity calls us to humility and caution. We are warned not to assume that our pet crusades are God's holy will. We are reminded that encoded images written in another time and place are open to misuse and abuse. When these images no longer assure us that God has heard our cry of anguish, but rather become the grounds for our own violent battle cry, then faithfulness calls us to self-examination and deep soul searching. We cannot rule out the possibility that we may find ourselves in a time when such clear divisions arise. Yet, before we dare to fight that battle, this literature also holds up for us a vision of the end that God desires. We must first purge our own vision of God's will in the furnace of God's word, before turning the word against another.

REVELATION 21:1-6
A NEW HEAVEN AND A NEW EARTH

In this beautiful text, we see that the vividness of the images of struggle within apocalyptic literature is only surpassed by the stirring vision of the new reality that God will finally establish. Over and against the parade of wars and disasters that march through history, God's representative dares to hope that God will act to bring about something totally new. When death seems to be an endless reality, God promises that a different kind of end awaits us. After the troubled people have been assured God is with them in their struggle, they are also promised that God has another word of hope. That word is Jesus the Christ, the same person who spoke to us in our last reading. He is the word made flesh. He comes and makes all things new, for the end of death comes in the one who is our beginning and our end. Jesus promises an end to the same old things that we know too well. Thanks to the gift he brings us, we shall end up in the embrace of God. Both heaven and earth, those realms that were shaken in the struggle, will be made new. The one who created "in the beginning" now recreates a holy people. The tyrants' death dealings will be swallowed up and brought to an end.

John, the one who writes this text and who sees the vision of God's future, proclaims many things about the reality that God is bringing to history. First, we hear that the gift is new. This does not simply mean that the gift is like the old we have known, only fresher, newness in this text implies something beyond all of our experience. We are surprised by the new life that we could not have even dreamed of on our own. This is not a mending job; all things are made new. Heaven and earth are transformed in their totality.

Next, the new reality is not created by human beings. This new creation is a gift of God. The earth does not produce the transformation through its own powers. Rather, the gift "comes down out of heaven from God" (Revelation 21:2). God alone has prepared it. Only when God is the sole source of this new gift can we be sure that it will not be freshened up oldness, like stale bread warmed up in the microwave. The mouth watering scent of home-baked bread just out of the oven awaits us at the banquet that God is preparing.

The new reality is not a private matter. Like a banquet or a worship service, the salvation God offers comes to the community of faith. Moreover, this community of faith is shaped by the word of good news that is announced to it. The new life for the community comes like a voice crying out, announcing the word of promise that God is with the people. This word is also not a human invention, but comes from God's own throne. The word does more than announce something already accomplished. As God speaks to the people about God's commitment to be with them, that relationship takes on flesh.

Thus the word itself does what it promises. The old fears that God had abandoned the people or that God neither listened to them nor cared about them are cast out as God speaks to them in the language of love and commitment. The shaken heavens are reestablished in the words from God's throne. God not only promises to be with the people, but God also promises, "You will be my people." The concerns and worries, the sins that we have committed and the sins committed against us, all that we throw up between God and ourselves, are knocked out of the way by the divine claim made upon us: "You are mine." Hearing this declaration of love, our hearts are taken captive by the one who speaks to us. We cease to trust in the false promises and menacing threats of others who have tried to crowd God and God's grace out of our lives. We trust in God, and thus we become God's people. Trust in the love and grace of God make us who we are by affirming *whose* we are. Trust in the love that comes as total gift makes us new.

This new love, handed over to the community of faith, brings the end of death. Of all the realities that haunt us, death strikes with a finality like no other. Death means an ending of life which, occasionally gently but more often brutally, cuts off all of our relationships.

Take June, for example. She was experiencing the worst two years of her life. Her husband died unexpectedly in an accident. Six months later, one of her children died of cancer. A year later, her best friend, the one who had stood with her at the two earlier funerals, died. To top all this off, her left hip needed replacement. She was worried that she would no longer be able to live in her home filled with so many crucial memories. As she saw these relationships slip from her grasp, she felt as though the world was falling down around her; even worse, it felt as though heaven itself was shaken. She found it hard to believe that God was her companion; she wondered where God's compassion and love had gone. In her relationship with her son, June knew love concretely; with her husband, she had learned what compassion was; and through her best friend's support, June had experienced divine companionship. But when all concrete signs of God's love were ripped away, how could she find faith again? Yet in the process of mourning within a community of faith, life slowly became new for her. She could trust that the God who held her loved ones also sustained her. Through the words spoken in her pastor's sermon, in the hopeful expressions of friends, and in stories shared, she began to feel alive again. As she received the consolation offered in the community of faith, June began to feel connected again to life, to her friends, and to God. Death began to be swallowed up by the word of life that God spoke to her through others.

June's trust in the promise of what God would do one day brought her a foretaste of that day in her hour of need. God's future embrace met her concretely in the word spoken and embodied among her brothers and sisters in Christ. June's trust in the word was not unlike that of Daniel struggling in El Salvador or like that of the writer of the text from Revelation that we have just read. Though they all knew the painful reality of death visited mercilessly upon them and their loved ones, they dared to trust in the mercy of the God revealed in Jesus Christ. They listened to the word of hope and believed. Though the evidence for the God of life did not present itself to their earthly eyes, their hearts of faith believed that God was trustworthy. And so they took the future as though it were already a present reality: "It is done" (Revelation 21:6). They trusted in the one who is the Alpha and the Omega, the beginning and the end of life. What happens in the end? The God of life happens to us!

Focus on the Stories

Think again about the stories of Daniel and June. They seem to live in two different worlds, and yet the same promises of God speak vividly to each.

◆ How would you define the struggles that Daniel has experienced in his life?

◆ How would you define the struggles that June has experienced in her life?

◆ What are the similarities and differences between their lives?

◆ Now think about struggles you have known in your own life. How are they similar to those of Daniel or June?

◆ What brought you—or is helping to bring you—through those difficult times?

◆ As Christians we are called to share each others burdens. How might you help bear the burdens of those who are suffering like June or Daniel?

Say a short prayer for a person in your Bible study group, addressing a concern she or he raised.

For the Next Session

During this next week think about whether you ever heard anyone talk about reincarnation or past lives that they have lived. What are your impressions of this?

Closing

God of life, be with us in our struggles. We pray especially for those who face (list the struggles shared in this session's gathering). Let them know that they are not alone in their strife and that you shall give them new life; in the name of Jesus Christ. Amen

Reincarnation

*While some believe our salvation
is to be our own achievement,
many Christians confess a gift
that is not earned.*

ROMANS 5:6-12
THE FREE GIFT

Sometimes the best way to understand yourself is to meet someone who is different. In face of this other, the things that distinguish you from each other and the things you share as humans both come into focus. In this session, we look at reincarnation in order to see the uniquely Christian understanding of salvation.

Reincarnation means to come into the flesh again. It refers to a process by which the souls of the dead enter into a new body, living another time on earth. Within this system of thought, your body houses a soul that has lived in other bodies. Within Hinduism, for example, this soul is attempting to move toward a salvation that is impossible to achieve in one life. The life you now live is the soul's second chance (or third, or fourth, and so on). Depending on the life you live, you may advance or demote the soul's status for its next trip through the flesh. The soul is graded according to the completion of one's social and religious duties. The process is automatic, based upon an already established scale of rewards and punishment. Your present placement is the soul's past performance record.

Christian faith might raise many objections to this understanding. We might recall in the last session that creation is not simply spinning around; God is taking it somewhere.

In Session 5, we will also be reminded that in the Bible both body and soul make up the self. The body is not unimportant to God. The body is part of who we are, not merely a container for our real self. These and other objections might be raised, but they are not the fundamental reason that a Christian cannot place his or her faith in reincarnation. The text from Romans brings us to the true heart of the matter.

This text is highly offensive to our human sensibilities. It declares that our relationship to God, both now and in the future, is founded not upon what we do, but upon the fact that God has sent Jesus Christ to reconcile us to God. Paul's language is not easy to understand. Part of the blame for this belongs to his difficult sentence structures. But even more, the difficulty lies in what he describes: the grace of God. This gift flies in the face of life as we normally know it.

Paul repeats numerous times in the text that our reconciliation with God is a "free gift." The fact that our relationship with God is a gift means that God alone gives it and that we have done nothing to earn it. Our reconciliation with God happens not because of who we are; rather, God's reconciliation often happens in spite of what we are. Our salvation comes not as our achievement, but as God's. Lest we try to claim even a tiny bit of credit, some little thing in us that draws God to our side, Paul uses the strongest terms he can find to name our condition in the presence of God outside of what Christ accomplishes

> **Fast Facts**
> Reincarnation is a belief within many world religions, such as Hinduism, Buddhism, and African ancestral and Australian aboriginal religions. Within North American popular culture, New Age spirituality often has adopted elements of this belief. In each of these, the understanding of reincarnation takes different forms, yet the belief that a soul passes through various bodies in the process of its eternal pilgrimage is shared by them all.

on the cross. We were ungodly people and sinners under the dominion of death and condemned by the law. Yet God chooses us precisely in that state so that the full glory might belong to God. God's glory is to give a gift wholly independent of our deserving it. We can be confident in the salvation that is ours only when we receive it as an all-out gift from God. Turn attention to ourselves, and we build our faith on shifting sands, losing the trust in God that God's grace offers.

By now the difference between the biblical witness and faith in the reincarnation should be clear. In the notion of reincarnation, our spiritual status relies upon our own achievement. Depending upon how we live, our souls either go forward or backward into the next reincarnation. If they move forward, this is because we have fulfilled the laws set down. How different this is than the biblical witness to a free gift! Our salvation is not dependent on a loveless system of law and our obedience to it, but is based on the love of a personal God who comes to us in Christ Jesus while we are yet ungodly. The logic of law is overcome by that of love. Systems of law, especially distant cosmic ones with no court of appeal, are impossible to love. We may respect them and do our best to obey them, but we do not love them. But a personal God, who loves us *so much* as to come to meet, save, and reconcile us, is completely different. This one we might love. Found in God's embrace, we know love. This divine lover invites our trust. We can live confidently in this embrace.

In reincarnation, we are ultimately cast back upon ourselves. No final assurance is offered. How can we know if we really did all that the cosmos requires of us? A contemporary music group, the Indigo Girls, muses upon reincarnation in a song entitled "Galileo." At one point the singer asks, "How long 'til my soul gets it right? Can any human being ever reach that kind of light?" Our future destiny remains precarious at best. The singer wonders if the sense of responsibility that reincarnation calls for might at least make us live more carefully, even lessening the chances of nuclear annihilation.

The apostle Paul also would not have us escape from our responsibility for the human choices that we make. Whether or not nuclear war occurs really does matter to God. Paul insists that the law makes appropriate demands upon us; the problem is that it does not provide the means to fulfill them. Only when we are freed from the claim that God's gift is our achievement are we finally ready to live in a way that does not harm our neighbor. Living in the reconciling embrace of God we are free to turn, without fear or anxiety, toward the task of living together humanely.

LUKE 15:11-32
RECKLESS GENEROSITY

U pon a first glance, this story might seem to be totally unre- lated to the question of whether the Bible says anything regarding reincarnation. Yet, remember from last week's session that final salvation in the Christian sense is about our relationship with God. When God's final will is accomplished, then God shall fully dwell with us and we shall be God's own people. God will have taken our hearts captive to divine love. We also might remember that one of the Bible's favorite images for God's great ending is a banquet. This story is about the journey to that ban- quet. Take a moment and examine this story of Jesus. Later, we will think about reincarnation again.

This story is best known under the title "The Prodigal Son." If this story were not around, the word *prodigal* would not even be known to most of us. *Prodigal* means recklessly extravagant or gen- erous. The familiar title reminds us of the way the son squandered his family's wealth. The fact that this son captures center stage in our imagination comes as no surprise; his action is so awful that we are ready to join the elder brother in criticizing him. He leaves his family at a time when they must have counted upon his help on the farm. He leaves his father and brother to bear more than their share of the labors, and he takes his inheritance with him. Half of the resources the father had to maintain the farm and his own life are given up to serve the whims of the son. This son treats his father as though he were already dead!

The son then goes out and spends his entire share of his father's lifetime of earnings in reckless living. Shouldn't the father have known he could not trust this son with so much? Surely this was not the first sign of his carelessness. The son squanders the father's gift and finds himself in the company of pigs. Pigs, of course, tell us how far this boy has wandered from his father's homeland. Pigs were considered unclean animals, which meant that Jesus' people, the Jews, would have nothing to do with them. This son is far gone, dining with swine on the garbage of others.

Finally, the story takes a positive turn. Or does it? The son finally examines himself, his recklessness, the harm he has done to his father, and decides to turn his life around. He vows to return to his father's home, confess his evil ways, and accept the status of a mere hired hand. This is the way religious folks normally want to hear the story. The older brother might suggest that something else is going on in his younger brother's heart.

Perhaps the younger son's heart has not turned at all. Maybe we are hearing only another variation on the same old line. The older brother might suggest that this scheming scoundrel has simply come up with one more way to play daddy's heart strings. Perhaps the son has undergone no moral turning at all. From what we know of him, this would not surprise us.

We could hear the story this way: The son comes to himself and realizes that dear old dad would certainly not turn him away if he did a little groveling. "Yeah, this will work," he might have thought. "I'll run up to dad and then, let's see, I'll fall at his feet. That will be nice for dramatic effect. Then I'll say something that will really get him, like, 'Father, I have sinned against heaven and before you.' That'll work, and I'll say, 'I am no longer worthy to be called your son; treat me like one of your hired hands.' Yes, sir, that's the ticket." And the son travels home to play one more trick on his father.

We will need to ask later on why we may prefer one of these ways of understanding the story over the other, but for now we will set that aside. The son goes home dragging his feet, maybe sincerely, maybe not. But finally that does not matter, at least not to the father. He sees his son while he is a far way off. Has he been watching and waiting since the day his son left? Seeing his boy, the father sprints to greet him full of compassion. Before the son can begin his well-rehearsed speech, the father is kissing and hugging him. When the son finally gets to make his speech we have no indication that the father even hears it. The father is busy calling out orders so that a celebration can take place. He insists on rings, robes, and sandals. He declares a banquet with the choicest fare to honor the son's return.

No wonder the older son is angry! He is not angry because his brother was prodigal; he is angry because his father is. Remember, *prodigal* means recklessly extravagant or generous. We understand why he is upset. He has been dedicated to his father's farm; if anyone has earned the inheritance, he has. Yet the one who has done nothing positive and everything negative is the one who is getting rewarded. The father shrugs. This does not change what the elder son will receive. He too can enjoy this generosity. Whoever said that receiving the inheritance had anything to do with earning it? Those are not the father's rules. His inheritance to his sons is a gift given freely on the basis of his love, not on the basis of the heirs' merits. Are we ready to believe that about the inheritance that God offers us? What holds us back from wanting or trusting that this is so? Are we ready to join in the party?

This resistance to the free gift offered by God discloses something important that we should not overlook. In the beginning of this session, we mentioned that encountering someone different can help us understand who we are. We see the differences between us that stand out, but also the similarities that remain in spite of the differences. The difference between the biblical view of salvation and that of faith in reincarnation is clear: Gift stands over and against achievement. But we have also come to observe something of the similarities that remain. Though the Bible speaks consistently of God's grace as free gift, we have come to see that in our day to day living, Christians also have a hard time believing that this should be so. We have our own faith in achievement and serve our own systems of law. In this sense, the pure gift of the gospel stands over and against the beliefs we hold in our hearts just as much as it stands in contradiction to those who believe in reincarnation. We too wish to find some claim from our side, no matter how small. Do we not at least turn to accept the gift? Is that not something? This story of the prodigal father reminds us that even the younger son did not choose to eat at the banquet. He was embraced by the reckless generosity and love of his father, and found himself swept into eating and celebrating that love before he even knew what was happening.

Focus on the Stories

Think about your response to the two ways of understanding the homeward journey of the son. Why is it that we may find ourselves looking for some reason, however small, that the son might be worthy of the father's embrace? What is the offense in the total giftedness of God's grace?

◆ Can you relate to the older brother? How about the younger one? Or have you ever felt like the father? Which one feels most familiar to you?

◆ Can you think of a time when you received a totally free gift? How did this feel?

◆ What are some examples of systems that we might look to in order to evaluate whether or not a person deserves to be loved and valued?

◆ In your congregation, do people ever act like their years of dedication should give them a preference over people who have just arrived in the church? How does this story challenge that attitude?

◆ What would be the difference in our lives if we really believed in our thoughts, words, and deeds that God's love is totally a gift, freely given? How would that change the way we see ourselves? How would that change the way we treat others?

For the Next Session
Think of one joke about heaven and hell that you can share next week.

Closing
Gracious God, you have gone to great lengths to reveal the total givenness of your gift. Capture our hearts in your love, rescuing us from our own bondage to achievement and merit; through your Son, Jesus Christ, our Lord. Amen

Heaven and Hell

The way we live matters for
eternity; we are called to faith
in God and faithfulness to others.

MATTHEW 18:1-14
ATTENTION TO THE LITTLE ONES

N o other aspect of the biblical witness has captured the
popular imagination as much as heaven and hell. The
belief that our lives lead into eternal destinies of punishment or
reward has been captured in some of the greatest art produced in
the West. Yet its impact is seen most clearly in the jokes we tell
each other over and over again. "A priest, a rabbi, and the presi-
dent all found themselves standing before St. Peter at the Pearly
Gates…" And off we go.

These jokes demonstrate how deeply the idea of a final judgment has entered our collective thinking. Yet, as intrigued as we
are by this notion, they also make equally clear that we are not
sufficiently interested in the testimony of the scriptures to get
what they are saying right.

Throughout this course, we have emphasized that our salvation and eternal destiny is God's gift, not our achievement. In
most jokes about heaven, the characters are judged on the basis of
what they have done. The one who has achieved well has earned
the highest score in St. Peter's accounting book and thus gets to
ride in a limo. The less successful end up on a skateboard or worse.

Another variation of the heavenly jokes are equally offensive to the biblical witness. In these, the one who tells the joke uses heaven as the setting to confirm God's support for his or her own personal prejudices. During football season, jokes are shared that demonstrate how God is backing "my" team. In our Father's house there are many mansions, but over them all flies "my" team's logo (whether that team be athletic, religious or racial).

We are ever capable of co-opting the theme of eternal judgment into our own favorite criteria for reward and punishment. This destroys the graciousness of the divine gift. There is perhaps only one joke that gets the biblical theme of God's graciousness. In all the rest, the kingdom of heaven becomes our own club, and with that club we will hit on the head anyone who says otherwise. Let us look at our session's first text as it speaks of "the kingdom of heaven" (Matthew 18:1) and "the hell of fire" (Matthew 18:9). We will study it carefully in order to truly understand God's judgments.

The text begins when the disciples ask Jesus which one of them is most important in the kingdom of heaven. No doubt some of them want to be confirmed as the clear leader, second only to Jesus himself. Other disciples, who may not hold hopes to be named the greatest, may wish to know whom they should imitate among the higher achievers. Imagine this circle of leaders waiting for Jesus' definitive ranking.

Jesus answers their question, but he certainly does not satisfy their pretensions to power. Jesus sees a little toddler playing nearby and calls the child into the circle of the great ones. Jesus holds the toddler who, no doubt, is unsure of what is going on and is a bit afraid of the intimidating circle she finds surrounding her. Yet she trusts the one who holds her. Jesus turns to the disciples and says that this trembling yet trusting child has it right! She makes no claims to power or authority in the kingdom of heaven. She is simply trusting in him. If they want to be great, they must "repent," or "turn around." In this case, repentance means turning back the clock in order to become trusting children again.

This, of course, is the one "joke" about eternity that gets it right! Unfortunately, the disciples do not seem to get it. They are so perplexed by this punch line that they do not laugh at its divine comedy. It has not gotten any easier for Christians since then to catch the truth inherent in Jesus' joke.

The followers of Jesus, then and now, are all too busy establishing their own authority to stop and see the gift offered. We are too busy with St. Peter's supposed accounting books to join in God's laughter. Yet the greatest act in the kingdom of heaven is trusting the one who holds us. With this trust, we finally abandon our own claims to worthiness. Sometimes, even when you do not really get a joke, you should laugh along with the one telling it. For as we echo Christ's laughter, we are caught up in his joy. Then we forget about ourselves long enough to glimpse the gift offered.

Hell's fire in this story is reserved for those who have stuck to their grim schemes of spiritual accounting. They threaten the child's trust in Christ's embrace by teaching accounting.

They do this in words, but also in actions. They live trusting in their own hands, in their own efforts. They look with their own eyes—they judge by human criteria. Thus the child learns not to trust in the divine gift, but to stray from it, seeking salvation by his own hands, judging with human eyes. Jesus says that it is better to cut off your hands or pluck out your eyes than to live like this forever.

Jesus also knows that where the judgments of human hands and eyes prevail, the child will be lost. In the seeking of power and prestige for themselves, in that human gaze looking ever upward, supposed great ones inevitably will step on the children. Jesus invites us to pay attention to the children. Accepting their example of trust, we accept the gift of Christ once again. We celebrate this gift with the one who goes out, not in search of the strong and well placed, but rather in search of the vulnerable little one.

JOHN 6:25-40
TRUST THE WORK OF GOD

The crowd who comes to Jesus in this story has just been fed by him. By the blessing of Jesus, a child's two sardines and five dinner rolls became a feast for thousands (John 6:1-14). The crowd has worked hard following Jesus to the other side of a lake, yet he accuses them of missing the point of that event. The miracle they experienced should not direct them to their bellies, but to that which will always matter. This is not to say that Jesus is unconcerned about the feeding of our bellies. After all, he was the one to perceive their physical hunger and to make sure that they were fed. But he wanted them to see the big picture, of which the miracle was only a part.

Jesus sets up a pair of contrasts in verse 26. On the one hand is the food they "work" for that "perishes"; on the other is the food the Son of Man (a title for Jesus) "will give" that "endures." The tension between human effort and divine gift again inserts itself into the biblical text.

The tension continues in verse 28 when, as the King James Version correctly puts it, the crowd asks, "What shall we do to work the works of God?" Jesus' response must have seemed strange to them. "This is the work of God, that you believe in him whom he has sent." The "work" that matters is "to believe" in Jesus, or as our last reflection put it, "to trust." Believing, or "faith," is the proper human response to the trustworthy presence of God revealed in Jesus. Yet even this human response is not finally the result of human effort. It is the

Fast Facts While worshiping, the church often confesses an ancient statement of faith, the Apostles' Creed. In that creed we state that between Jesus' crucifixion and resurrection he "descended into hell." This phrase stresses the extent to which Jesus was willing to enter into the depths of human lostness. Jesus went to hell—the utmost extreme—in order to proclaim the message of God's love for sinners. (See 1 Peter 3:19; 4:6 and Ephesians 4:9.)

"work of God." Finally, not the work we do, but the faith that God works in us is what matters for eternity.

Jesus is the one who has "come down from heaven" (John 6:32, 33, 38) as we have already learned in Session 1. Doing so, he gives life to the world (John 6:32). He satisfies that ever-present hunger and thirst for something more. He is "the bread of life" (John 6:35) in whom we have eternal life (John 6:40).

Jesus' listeners might have thought that they were being invited to do too little. Is faith or trust all that is really required? Anyone who has lived and reflected on their life knows that trusting totally in God's gift does not come easy. We cannot in and of ourselves somehow come up with trust in God. Something or someone has to interrupt our fears and anxieties so that trust can be born in us.

Take the example of three-year-old Kayla. She was rambunctious while her mom prepared to marry Steve. Throughout the wedding rehearsal Kayla was drawing all attention to herself. At the ceremony, she continued her wildness, playing hide and seek behind the communion rail. One thought churned through her, "Will I have a place in this new family?" Then in the middle of the wedding something happened that changed her. She saw her mom and Steve kneeling beside her. They each hugged her and promised, "You will always have a place in our home; you are our beloved child!" With these words all Kayla's wildness was tamed. She stepped back calm and content. She finally allowed everyone else to focus on God's joining of her mother and Steve.

When we are not sure that we have a place in God's family, a wildness takes possession of us, and we seek to draw all attention to ourselves. Something needs to happen that will quiet our fears. Therefore, God in Christ has come down beside us. He comes to us today and promises, "I have prepared a place for you; your space in God's eternal embrace is secure." All that is left for us is to trust him. We can cease to call attention to ourselves and simply serve the larger event in which we are but a part.

Kayla's story reminds us that trust comes from meeting one who is shown to be trustworthy. She did not come up with the trust on her own. Trust was inspired by the caring presence of others. Likewise, our faith in God is inspired by God's intervention through Christ. Listening to the stories of his life, of his acceptance of the little ones, and his love on their behalf, we meet Christ. He also promises to be present for us in the meal we share in his name. He promises that he gives us himself, the bread of life, so that we might never be hungry again. In this meal, we eat with Jesus in hope of the final heavenly banquet.

Draw together what has been learned thus far about "What happens in the end?" Recall from Session 2 that God's final victory is the gift of gracious divine presence. This final victory is what we call heaven or the kingdom of heaven. We await this day in faith, longing for the fullness of God's will to be manifest. This future reality is ours today in Christ. The "bread of life" feeds us as we trust that he is the source of life.

If the kingdom of heaven is about our trust in the relational presence of God, then hell is the opposite. Hell is our lack of trust in God's gracious presence as well as the broken relationship that this implies. Where God is not trusted, there we know only condemnation or false security. Cut off from the source of life, we experience the total brutality of death.

While Christians know of eternal judgment, we must pay attention daily to God's criteria in that judgment. We must not forget that according to the Bible, heaven is not made for moral or spiritual superstars, but for the lost whom Jesus finds and takes with him. If one is worried about hell, the best act is to lean on Jesus and his promise of eternal life. This focus not only turns our minds to other things, but turns us over into God's kingdom as trust is again inspired in us.

If one is worried about another lost soul, the best thing we can do is bring them to meet the one whom we have come to trust. We do this when we tell them the story of Jesus, when we bring them to worship where God again comes down to meet us, when we accept and serve them with the love of Christ.

Though Christians accept the testimony of the Bible that there will be an eternal separation, in our heart of hearts we hope that God will ultimately have the victory not only for us, but for the whole world. At times, the Bible also gives testimony to an all-out victory won by God in which even hell's separation is vanquished and God is all in all. We recall in our first session that we hope for a day when "every" knee should bend, and "every" tongue confess faith in Jesus Christ (see Philippians 2:10, 11). Though how this total victory can be reconciled with the other testimony to the existence of hell is a mystery, we trust that the mystery will ultimately be resolved by the gracious God we know in Christ. The mystery that will one day triumph over us can be trusted to be none other than the mystery of God's love.

Focus on the Stories

Think about the person whom you trust most in all the world. Finish this sentence in relation to them: I trust in

_____ because

_____.

Now without changing the second blank, change the first to "Jesus." Does the sentence still make sense? How is it that Jesus is like the people we have come to trust? How does his trustworthiness even surpass their trustworthiness? What are the ways that we learn of Christ's trustworthiness?

◆ Remember how you came to trust another person? Was it easy or difficult? Have you ever felt a freedom like Kayla knew once she trusted that she was a part of the family? How did that confidence change you and your life's activities?

◆ Since you do not have to do anything but trust in God's graciousness in order to be a part of God's kingdom, what would you like to do in service to your neighbor? Imagine how you might reshape your little corner of the world so that it starts to reflect the kingdom of heaven.

◆ If someone asked you if you were going to heaven or hell, how might you respond to him or her?

◆ What is it that you most hunger and thirst for in life? Are these things "perishable" or "enduring" (see John 6:27)?

◆ Jesus fed the people physically and then called upon them to examine their deeper hungers. Why does Jesus take both of these needs seriously? What do you think is the relationship between these two kinds of hunger?

◆ How might trusting in God's grace affect the way that you understand yourself? How might that same trust affect the way you treat others?

For the Next Session
Think about a baptism in which you participated. You might call to mind your own baptism or that of another.

Closing
Eternal God, teach us to trust in your graciousness. Let us so focus on your Son, Jesus, that we are inspired to place all of our concerns about today on you. Help us to trust that we shall dwell in the mystery of your love forever. In your name we pray. Amen

The Resurrection

God comes to us in the shadow
of death, calling our name and
bringing us new life in Christ.

JOHN 20:11-18
GRACIOUS NAME CALLING

Mary does what people have done for ages. She goes to the place where the person whom she loved had been laid to rest. She goes to feel some meager sense of connection to what had been. She goes to remember what now seemed to be a distant past. She probably goes with low expectations, hoping mostly for distraction from her grief.

In the morning, when she arrives at the tomb, it appears that even her small hope will be destroyed. She goes to the tomb and finds that his body has been taken. Insult is added to injury. Who would have done such a thing? She begs those present to show a little humanity, to tell her where the body of the one that she loved has been taken. She turns around and sees another man, probably the gardener. He calls her "woman" and shows her compassion, but she is not turned from her quest to find the precious cadaver. "Sir," she responds, "just tell me where you have put him, please." But when the "gardener" calls her by name, "Mary," she is turned around—and so is her world. She responds to his name, sighing, "Teacher." She runs to his arms and takes hold of him. At last, things can be like they once were! Jesus gently warns her that this is not so. He removes himself from her tight embrace. "No, Mary, things cannot be like they were, but they will be so much better! Now I have places that I must go. Do not hold me back to what I once was. God has so much more in mind. Tell the others that I will go to my Father whom now you can claim with total confidence as your Father; I go to my God who has become your God as well." And Mary runs away, transformed, to announce the good news.

Mary came to the tomb, hoping to connect with her past in some small way. Instead, a whole new future was opened up for her. When Jesus called her by name she was transformed and recognized that what had been lost was now found. Once Jesus helped her see the meaning of this encounter, she had to share that news with others.

The good news that Jesus was raised from the dead became the message that had to be shared by those who had followed him. His resurrection was the message of the good news, but it was also the power that drove the faithful to announce the event. The risen Christ inspired the trust needed to proclaim that God is trustworthy.

To understand the resurrection of Jesus, we must also remember his life and death. Jesus died as one condemned by both political and religious authorities. The highest courts in the land had decided that he was guilty, that his message was wrong, and that his identity was false. There was no higher court in the land to which his followers could appeal. Jesus' life and teachings, therefore, were all called into question. He had claimed that God was a friend of sinners, that God stood by those suffering in the

Fast Facts The resurrection stories in the gospels all claim that women first announced Jesus' resurrection. The male disciples had a hard time accepting this. In one account, some male followers of Jesus find themselves walking with the risen Jesus without recognizing him. When they tell of the women's testimony which they cannot believe, Jesus says, "Oh, how foolish you are, and how slow of heart to believe all that the prophets have declared!" (Luke 24:25). A double meaning is implied!

shadow of death, and that God would show mercy on those forsaken by others. His condemnation and execution was not only a public accusation of error, it was itself the proof that he was wrong. He died like a sinner and was shown no mercy. He hung there for all to see, clearly condemned and forsaken by God. He and his teaching were nothing after all.

When there was no higher court in all of the land to reverse this verdict, God acted in order to raise Jesus Christ from the dead! This act of God overthrows the opinion of the human courts and reverses them. The one who was named false is true; the one who seemed forsaken by God is actually the bearer of God to the whole world; the one who appeared to have nothing has everything in his hands. The judgment of the world has been reversed, for God has spoken.

Notice that in the resurrection of Jesus, more is happening than the bringing to life of a dead man. The importance of this miraculous transformation is not only that a dead man lives, but that a particular dead man, Jesus Christ, has been raised from the dead. God has declared publicly that Jesus got it all right! The future is in God's hands and not ours. God will make us into God's own people. Wandering and derelict heirs are welcomed home by God with reckless celebration. The toddler is the model member of this kingdom. Trust is what God requires of us. Jesus taught all these things in his lifetime; God confirmed them in the resurrection. The resurrection of Jesus is the best proof of what Jesus had been trying to teach us about the kind of God we have.

Because Jesus had been raised, his followers came to know that they too would be resurrected. They were caught up in his Holy Spirit and believed that his destiny was also theirs, just as his God had become their God.

To this day, the church continues to hope that as Christ was raised from the dead, so also will all be raised who trust in his name. We now stand by our own loved ones' tombs, not seeking a small consolation, but boldly declaring that they shall be raised into the gracious presence of God. We hope for the total renewal of all that they are—body, soul, and spirit—recalling that Jesus rose bodily and not as a pure spirit. During those hard times by the grave, we long to be joined to all the faithful, including our dearly departed friends. We shall trust that our longing will be fulfilled. For the one who holds them seeks to hold our attention long enough so that we hear this divinely spoken promise. Our name, too, has been called, and nothing will ever be the same.

ROMANS 6:3-11
DYING AND RISING WITH CHRIST

The one who met Mary and called her by name promises to meet us in specific events in our lives. The first of these events, for many of us, is called baptism. Within the Lutheran • church, most of the faithful, though certainly not all, have been baptized as little children. This is done in good faith that such a "little one" is indeed the greatest in the kingdom of heaven as Jesus promised (see Matthew 18:1-14). Yet the utter charm of the scene may cause us to forget the serious event that is occurring. Something is happening that may not be picked up by our video recorders.

When the apostle Paul wanted to explain what happens in baptism, he spoke of a dying and rising with Christ. In baptism, we hear God call our name to claim us. We, like Mary in our last text, are given the gift of a new future. We, again like Mary, die to our despair and lack of ability to trust God. God comes and claims us while we have no claims of our own to make. We die to the desire to achieve our own salvation, for the gift is simply given. We die to the legion of voices that meet us each day with their multitude of demands. We rise to the place where we live according to God's voice. God stops us in our meager attempts to muster up a molecule of hope in order to offer newness totally beyond the scope of our old dreams. We die to the accusations of those who would judge us somehow wrong, and we rise together with Christ to that highest court where we are declared just for Jesus' sake.

Becoming a Christian does not always happen by birth into a Christian family. As an adult, a person might be so struck by the story of Jesus, his life, death, and resurrection, that she finds herself trusting in the God revealed and wants to commit her life to God's kingdom.

In the early church, the baptism that marked her turning was dramatic. On the eve of Easter morning, she would gather with others who had received months of intensive training in God's story. The priest would ask them all to turn toward the west, the direction from which the night comes. Staring the night in the face they would be asked three questions. First: "Do you renounce the devil?" And they would respond, "Yes," and spit literally into the darkness, "we renounce him." Then: "Do you renounce his evil works?" And they would again spit at the darkness and renounce. And they replied in the same way to the third question: "Do you renounce all the devil's empty promises?" They spat in the face of the devil as if to say, "Your promises leave only a bitter taste in our mouths!"

Then the priest would have them turn and face east, the place from which the sun rises. They would look toward the light which had shined on Mary's face that resurrection morning. They would again answer three questions, "Do you believe in God the Father?" "Yes, I believe..." "Do you believe in God the Son?" "Yes, I believe..." "Do you believe in God the Holy Spirit?" "Yes, I believe..." They turned from the empty promises of the king of liars toward the God who raised Jesus Christ from the dead by the power of the Holy Spirit. This done, they were dunked under water in the name of God: Father, Son, and Holy Spirit. Their names became wrapped up in the mystery of God's most holy name. Their lives could never be the same again.

Though our service may be a bit short on drama, God promises to be there nevertheless, bringing the same gifts to us as to those baptized almost two millennia ago. We are given the sign of God's promise that can turn us from death toward the new resurrection day.

By now you should know what is coming. Our future meets us in the waters of baptism. We are given the promise of incorporation into Christ. The glorious future relationship with God is already ours, though the video cameras might miss this important fact. We have been raised "so we too might walk in newness of life." We are raised to walk the way that Jesus walked. Our lives are no longer our own; they are God's!

How then shall we live, if we are already so accepted? What does newness of life look like? We know what that newness is when we look at Jesus. He was rightly called the Son of Man, the Truly Human One. He reveals to us the rhythms of newness in all that he says and does.

Jesus taught us to trust in God, for our daily bread and for our eternal salvation. He has made it clear that *God comes to us* so we do not have to search for God's graciousness through our own achievements. Having been freed from the need to earn God's favor, we turn in search of those around us who are in need. We look to those "little ones" whose lives are at risk, and we do what is necessary so that abundant life might be theirs.

We are freed from all that might enslave us: our self-centeredness, greed, possessions, the tyranny of others, and our past. We are freed in order to serve the neighbor in need. The resurrection is not only to be recalled at a loved one's grave. The resurrection is to be the mark of our lives each and every day. While all appearances may suggest that death has the final word, we trust in another word that meets us in the water of baptism. We trust that in those waters we have died to death and that the night no longer has the power to threaten us with its bullies. We turn together to anticipate the new reality that God is preparing for us, trusting that God will be our guide until we reach our end.

This means that the resurrection does not pull us out of our earthly existence, but rather draws us deeper into it. Through the gift of the resurrection we are drawn into an immense community much larger than anything we would ever dream up on our own. This is called "the communion of saints." We are joined to all those from every time and place whom Christ claimed as his own.

We are joined to those faithful who followed Jesus in his earthly walk almost two thousand years ago, and we are brought together with centuries of saints who have trusted in God from that time until now. We are joined with living Christians in Asia, Latin America, Eastern Europe, Africa, and around the whole globe. And we are brought into communion with those who have yet to live. What's more, we are brought into relation with the whole of creation that God sustains and will one day transform, together with us, in that final new creation.

While we await the new heaven and new earth where God will rule openly and plainly, we direct our lives toward these eternal companions. We seek to anticipate the healing that God will definitively bring in the end. We allow service to our neighbors to be the end toward which we live.

Focus on the Stories

Ysaye Maria Barnwell sings with an amazing African American women's a cappella group. In one song that she wrote, Barnwell tells of the role her grandmother, or her Nana, played in her life. This is the chorus to "No Mirrors in My Nana's House."

> There were no mirrors in my Nana's house
> No mirrors in my Nana's house
> And the beauty that I saw in everything,
> The beauty in everything
> Was in her eyes.
> (Warner Bros. Records, 1993)

In the loving gaze of her Nana, Ysaye received a foundational sense of who she was. Later in life, when she encountered the race hatred that so often reigns outside of her grandmother's house, she leaned upon that other vision to sustain her understanding of her own beauty as well as the beauty of all creation.

In the experience of her Nana's beautiful gaze, Ysaye knew that she was beautiful. One fruit of this wisdom given to her by her Nana was this beautiful song. The song brings the love full circle by declaring the beauty of Nana's gift and thus of Nana herself.

◆ In what way is the God who meets us in baptism "our Nana"? How is baptism the way that God establishes the beautiful household of faith?

◆ How might baptism offer an alternative interpretation to people who are disregarded by the world around them? Think of how faith in God sustained African American people through slavery, lynchings, and other forms of racist attacks. How does this experience make the reality of the apostle Paul's death/life contrast very concrete?

◆ Which groups in society are consistently told by the social mirrors on the wall (the assumed criteria of beauty and goodness) that they are ugly? How might those among us who are attacked in this way respond in light of our baptism? How might those among us who are favored by such appraisals (for example, people whose skin is white) respond in light of our baptism? What must die in all of us?

For the Next Session
Reflect on the whole course and be prepared to share what strikes you as most important.

Closing
God of love, in the waters of baptism you have brought about the death of death and have given us new life. Help us to live as a resurrected people, empowered by your grace to serve all those in need; in Jesus' name. Amen

Our Future Grounded in Christ

In the love of Christ, God's gracious future comes to us today, defining our present identity for us.

2 CORINTHIANS 6:1-10
TODAY: THE END AND THE BEGINNING

Paul has just written to the church at Corinth about the gift of reconciliation in Christ (see 2 Corinthians 5:16-21). He has told them of the new creation they are in Christ (5:17). He has begged them to see the world, themselves, and God from the perspective that the risen Christ revealed, and not from a typical human perspective (5:16). He has promised them that Christ was made a sinner so they would be made righteous (5:21). And he has called them as people who have been reconciled in Christ to be "ambassadors" (5:20) in "the ministry of reconciliation" (5:18).

Having pointed out the great gifts and ministry which are theirs, he urges them not to forget what he has been teaching. He begs them, "Do not accept the grace of God in vain" (6:1). Paul has shared with them the good news of Jesus Christ, and now he urges them not to forget what they have learned. Paul wants them to hold tightly to God and to remember that God is trustworthy. Paul is worried that the trust—pure and simple trust—that they have shown in Christ might be replaced with something else.

So Paul returns to the scriptures. In 2 Corinthians 6:2, he quotes a promise that God made long ago through the prophet Isaiah (see Isaiah 49:8). But then he says, "See, now is the acceptable day; see, now is the day of salvation!" (2 Corinthians 6:2) On behalf of God, Paul urges his friends to see that salvation is theirs now, not in some distant past or even only in the future. Today is their day! As this course comes to a close, the plea is the same: trust in God. For today is the day of your salvation!

Focus on the Story

Many things that we learn in our lives are soon forgotten. Forgetting is a natural part of being human. Yet there are some things that we dare not forget, for we will be miserable if we do not recall them. You will not suffer much if you no longer remember what *prolepsis* or *apocalyptic* means, though it would be wonderful if they have become part of the way that you now sort through your thoughts about God.

Yet, if you forget that God is gracious, if you forget the gift that Christ gives you, then the cost is indeed great. These things are easy to lose sight of in our daily lives. Thus we gather weekly in worship to hear God's word, to share God's meal, to celebrate among God's people, so that we might never forget.

◆ When Paul had asked his readers not to "accept the grace of God in vain" (6:1) what do you think that he meant?

◆ What are some of the most important things that you have learned to accept in this course? What would it mean for you not to "accept these things in vain"?

◆ How has your answer to the question "What happens in the end?" evolved in light of the scriptures and conversations of the last six sessions? Describe what emotions you feel when you think about the end? What surprises did you find in this course?

Closing

Gracious God, we give you thanks that today is the day of our salvation. Teach us not to fear the end of life, but to find our end and purpose in you; through your Son, Jesus Christ our Lord. Amen

How the Bible Is Organized

The Bible is divided into two "testaments." The Old Testament, which was originally written in Hebrew, contains four major sections that include 39 individual books. The New Testament, which was originally written in Greek, is divided into three sections that include 27 books.

THE OLD TESTAMENT

The Pentateuch
Genesis
Exodus
Leviticus
Numbers
Deuteronomy
History
Joshua
Judges
Ruth
1 and 2 Samuel
1 and 2 Kings
1 and 2 Chronicles
Ezra
Nehemiah
Esther
Wisdom
Job
Psalms
Proverbs

Ecclesiastes
Song of Solomon
Prophets
Isaiah
Jeremiah
Lamentations
Ezekiel
Daniel
Hosea
Joel
Amos
Obadiah
Jonah
Micah
Nahum
Habakkuk
Zephaniah
Haggai
Zechariah
Malachi

THE NEW TESTAMENT

The Gospels
Matthew
Mark
Luke
John
History
Acts of the Apostles
The Letters
Romans
1 and 2 Corinthians
Galatians
Ephesians

Philippians
Colossians
1 and 2 Thessalonians
1 and 2 Timothy
Titus
Philemon
Hebrews
James
1 and 2 Peter
1, 2, and 3 John
Jude
Revelation

Adapted from A *Beginner's Guide to Reading the Bible* by Craig R. Koester, copyright © 1991 Augsburg Fortress.

How to Read the Bible

FINDING A BIBLE REFERENCE

1. Check the Bible's table of contents if you do not know where the book is.

PSALM 119:105		
book of Bible	chapter	verse

2. In your Bible, the chapter numbers are large numbers, usually at the beginning of paragraphs. The chapter numbers might be also printed at the top of each page.
3. The verse numbers are tiny numbers, usually printed at the beginning of sentences.

UNDERSTANDING WHAT YOU READ

As you read a passage of the Bible, keep in mind these three questions:
1. What does this text tell me about God?
2. What does this text tell me about the people of God?
3. What does this text tell me about myself?

GOING DEEPER

Other questions that might help you understand what you are reading include:
1. What type of literature is this passage? Is it a story? A historical account? Poetry? A hymn? A letter? How might that affect my understanding of the passage?
2. What is the historical situation of the writer?
3. Who is speaking in this passage?
4. Who is being addressed in this passage? How am I like or different from that person or group?
5. How does the passage relate to the surrounding text? Does the surrounding material shed any light on the passage's meaning?
6. What are the key words and phrases in the passage? Which ones do I not understand?
7. How does the passage compare to parallel passages or to texts on the same subject?
8. What in the passage puzzles, surprises, or confuses me?

"Going Deeper" and "Marking Your Bible" are adapted from *Bible Reading Handbook* by Paul Schuessler, copyright © 1991 Augsburg Fortress.

Luther Says...

I. GOD'S WORK AS FATHER/CREATOR

The first article [of the Creed] teaches that God is the Father, the creator of heaven and earth. What is this? What do these words mean? The meaning is that I should believe that I am God's creature, that he has given to me body, soul, good eyes, reason, a good wife, children, fields, meadows, pigs, and cows, and besides this, he has given to me the four elements, water, fire, air, and earth. Thus this article teaches that you do not have your life of yourself, not even a hair. I would not even have a pig's ear, if God had not created it for me. Everything that exists is comprehended in that little word "creator." Here we could go on preaching at length about how the world, which also says, I believe in God, believes this. Therefore everything you have, however small it may be, remember this when you say "creator," even if you set great store by it. Do not let us think that we have created ourselves, as the proud princes think.

Luther's Works, vol. 51, *Sermons I*, edited and translated by John W. Doberstein (Philadelphia: Fortress Press, 1959), 162-163.

II. CHRIST'S WORK

On Galatians 2:19, "For I through the Law died to the Law, that I might live to God."

Thus with the sweetest names Christ is called my Law, my sin, and my death, in opposition to the Law, sin, and death, even though in fact He is nothing but sheer liberty, righteousness, life, and eternal salvation. Therefore He became Law to the Law, sin to sin, and death to death, in order that He might redeem me from the curse of the Law, justify me, and make me alive.... Thus Christ is a poison against the Law, sin, and death, and simultaneously a remedy to regain liberty, righteousness, and eternal life.

Luther's Works, vol. 26, *Lectures on Galatians, 1535, Chapters 1–4*, edited by Jaroslav Pelikan (Saint Louis: Concordia Publishing House, 1963), 163.

III. THE HOLY SPIRIT'S WORK

The third article [of the Creed], therefore, is that I believe in the Holy Spirit, that is, that the Holy Spirit will sanctify me and is sanctifying me.... How does he sanctify me? By causing me to believe that there is one, holy church through which he sanctifies me, through which the Holy Spirit speaks and causes the preachers to preach the gospel. The same he gives to you in your heart through the sacraments, that you may believe the Word and become a member of the church. He begins to sanctify now; when we have died, he will complete this sanctification through both "the resurrection of the body" and "the life everlasting."

Luther's Works, vol. 51, *Sermons I,* edited and translated by John W. Doberstein (Philadelphia: Fortress Press, 1959), 168.

IV. ESCHATOLOGY

The significance of baptism is a blessed dying unto sin and a resurrection in the grace of God, so that the old man, conceived and born in sin, is there drowned, and a new man, born in grace, comes forth and rises…. This significance of baptism—the dying or drowning of sin—is not fulfilled completely in this life…. For sin never ceases entirely while the body lives…. There is no help for the sinful nature unless it dies and is destroyed with all its sin. Therefore the life of a Christian, from baptism to the grave, is nothing else than the beginning of a blessed death. For at the Last Day, God will make him altogether new.

Luther's Works, vol. 35, *Word and Sacrament I,* edited by E. Theodore Bachman (Philadelphia: Fortress Press, 1960) 30-31.

V. FREEDOM OF A CHRISTIAN

Now that the question is raised, we must have a look at the nature of Christian freedom. Christian or evangelical freedom, then, is a freedom of conscience which liberates the conscience from works. Not that no works are done, but no faith is put in them…. Christ has freed this conscience from works through the gospel and teaches this conscience not to trust in works, but to rely only on his mercy….

And so, the conscience of a man of faith depends solely and entirely on the works of Christ. The conscience may be likened to the dove resting in safety in the clefts of the rock and in the secret places [Song of Sol. 2:14]. Such a soul knows with absolute certainty that it can have neither confidence nor peace except in Christ alone, and that in its own works nothing but guilt, fear, and condemnation can abide.

Luther's Works, vol. 44, *The Christian in Society,* edited by James Atkinson (Philadelphia: Fortress Press, 1966), 298-299.